HIDDEN VOICE PUBLISHING

Hidden Voice Publishing is an independent publishing resource centre that supports & represents authors from under-represented groups with publishing paperback and Amazon Kindle books.

HIDDEN VOICE PUBLISHING

ANTHOLOGY: VOLUME 2
2020

Published in 2020
Hidden Voice Publishing
www.hiddenvoicepublishing.co.uk

Edited By: Sarah Pritchard & Joel Sadler-Puckering

Cover Art By: Caroline Bradbury-Cheetham
Enquiries: mrscbc_50 on Instagram

"When the whole world is silent, even one voice becomes powerful.' Malala

Dedicated to the voiceless in 2020.

TITLES ON HIDDEN VOICE PUBLISHING

I KNOW WHY THE GAY MAN DANCES
JOEL SADLER-PUCKERING

INKY BLACK WOMAN
MINA AIDOO

FERAL ANIMALS
JOEL SADLER-PUCKERING

WHEN WOMEN FLY
SARAH PRITCHARD

HIDDEN VOICE: ANTHOLOGY VOLUME 1
VARIOUS AUTHORS

HIDDEN VOICE: ANTHOLOGY VOLUME 2
VARIOUS AUTHORS

FOREWORD

2020. Who could have imagined this real life post-apocalyptic dystopian like year?

Communal closeness, random intimacies, intergenerational hugs have become outlawed and in their place isolation, surgical masks, lockdown, conspiracies, a culling of our elders, countless others and the loss of freedoms.

Some, already on the edge of freedom & looking in, have said: Welcome to Our World.

How have we survived? How do we continue to be creative, to love, to speak our truths, even in the darkest of moments? The writers within these pages demonstrate, I believe, with determination, dedication and lived love, how to prevail. They have proudly unlocked their tongues, unfucked their heads, unpatholigised their feelings and imaginations into these flowers of freedom.

There may be wars & viruses. But who will stand up, push back even harder through the closet door of oppression, if not the brave, poor artist? I celebrate the special, extra push to be visible & be true to ourselves demonstrated here, especially in 2020.

Sarah Pritchard
(Editor of Hidden Voice Anthologies Volume 1 & 2)

CONTRIBUTERS

HIDDEN VOICE PUBLISHING

ANTHOLOGY: VOLUME 2

REBECCA AUDRA SMITH 15
MEDITATION ON BREATH
WE ARE NOT RACHEL AND KATE

RUTH BROOME 17
'UGHH'
EDGES

CATHY BRYANT 19
GRAFFITI
MERMAIDS DON'T DIE OF THIRST
WHAT THE SIRENS SANG TO ODYSSEUS

SARAH L DIXON 27
I AM THE CURATOR OF THE LOST THINGS.
FINDING THE QUIET
DANDELION GODDESS VISITS CHATHAM LIBRARY

ALETHA FIELDS 31
HYON
ON COOKING, BLACKNESS AND PLANTATIONS
THEY STILL DO IT

JOLIVIA GASTON 38
NOT OUR CHOICE
SEEDS OF MALICE
BABY

ELIZABETH GIBSON 42
WHY I USUALLY LIKE BEING QUEER
CÉLINE AT CANNES
FEED

MO HARROP 45
DONALD THE DANGEROUS
MY IMAGINATION

L.C. JANE 47
WHO CARES
TWO LIVES

ADY LAMB 49
KEYWORKER: COVID 19 ODE

ELLIE ROSE MCKEE 51
LAST BEING FIRST
WINGMAN

ANN MORGAN 59
MASKS

PAULINE OMOBOYE 60
A WOMAN'S RIGHT
CUT & DRY

SARAH PRITCHARD 63
PRIDE KIDS
WHEN YOU COME OUT, YOUR WHOLE FAMILY COMES OUT WITH YOU
UNLOCKDOWN

JOEL SADLER-PUCKERING 66
FRIDAY 13ᵀᴴ
DEAR ALAN
THE HUMANITARIAN AND THE FIRE EATER

PHIL TONGUE 69
NO BANANA SPLIT
TAKE IT IN YOUR STRIDE

LOUISE VEE 71
JUST SOME OF THE THINGS, I HAVE DISCOVERED,
THAT CANNOT STOP YOU HAVING A(NOTHER)
MISCARRIAGE

ANASTASIA VOROBYEVA 73
BECOMING BROKEN OPEN

STEVEN WALING 80
CREPUSCULE WITH NICA
INTO THE WOODS
KIRKYARD CAT

CARSON WOLFE 86
BUTCHES CAN'T WEAR SKIRTS

MANTZ YORK 88
A GRADUATE'S LAMENT
TRICKLE-DOWN ECONOMICS

REBECCA AUDRA SMITH

MEDITATION ON BREATH

*

The battle of normality and the bursting of the balloons when we use our breath to blow them up and on Sundays when the bell tolls we make gay love

*

What enters our lips
And what exits.
We consume and expel like magic.

How gay am I? How queer am I?
As queer as the bell that tolls?
As queer as love in bed on Sundays;

she smiles at you and tickles your ribs,
he leans over to kiss your face,
they slide their hand to clasp your flesh

As tenderly as slicing a lamb.

They slide their hand to clasp your flesh
He leans over to kiss your face
She smiles at you and tickles your ribs

As queer as love in bed on Sundays
As queer as the bell that tolls
How gay I am, how queer I am

We consume and expel like magic
And what exits
What enters our lips.

WE ARE NOT RACHEL AND KATE

I've been a lesbian 44 years.

Although we are lesbians and we do mate
We did not bring a u-haul to the second date
Or the third. We are not Rachel and Kate.

She is her and I am me and together we are we
Not tied at the wrist or the ring finger and we try
Not to look like each other and it's simple to be gay

As simple as naming your club G.A.Y
As simple as naming your star sign
as simple as owning a cat

We like to bake bread, we like to plan ahead
But our names are not blended or mingled or fried
And when we make the beast with two backs we are still

Ourselves, flowing into our skins, tingling in our ears
My eyes closed and hers open and we are not the same person
And what I said earlier is a lie

It is not simple to be gay, coming out like repetitively opening
and closing a door. Try it! Let's try endlessly
Crossing from one side to another

With no real difference except the air's temperature
Is hotter, and your breath comes faster, and now, you are gay
and you're inside a club named G.A.Y

RUTH BROOME

'UGH'

You appear by the coffee machine
contemplative soft brown eyes
flicking to my green pools
hovering there
darting away
returning
once more
an overture

Ugh

EDGES

Edges I

Her
lythe body beneath my hands
searching for recognition
'no god damn hair'
but on her head
migrated
there

Edges II

Him
skin stretched across
beer bare belly
ash blonde
chalk grey curls
I long to walk a thousand miles through

Edges III

her light flicks
his wet wet tongue
his hard
her soft
edges

CATHY BRYANT

GRAFFITI

Jo had been sent to the shop with exactly the right money for his cigarettes. If the price had gone up and she went home without them, Jo's husband would hit her. So she hoped that they were still on offer.

A tag was bright on the wall she walked beside. JACK, in yellow and orange, unashamed sun-colours. Jo imagined being Jack, and seeing herself as something colourful to share with the world. Yellow, orange. She never wore them. Just the dark, baggy clothes that Simon picked out for her.

"You're too old for bright colours," he explained. "And you don't have the figure. You'd look like an old whore."

That was after he'd thrown out her favourite dress. It was a soft blue and Jo had felt happy in it.

Now, without realising, Jo had stopped in front of the tag.

"Graffiti. Disgusting," Simon always said. "They're animals. They should be birched."

I'm just glad that someone, somewhere, isn't ashamed of who they are, thought Jo.

She smiled at Jack's tag.

It smiled back.

The colours curved at the ends, and Jack was now grinning at her.

Oh great. Now I'm going mad.

But it wasn't scary and it didn't feel wrong. Jo had a sense of friendship and understanding.

She blinked away the tag, and trudged on through the greyness of wet streets.

Sanjeev's shop was brightly lit and he smiled a welcome. It hadn't occurred to Simon that Jo might be friendly with the owner. Naturally Simon was racist as well as everything else, and he assumed that Jo, as a white person, would be too.

But Jo smiled at Sanjeev. "Twenty Bensons, please," she said. "How's Pritti?"

"As pretty as her name and as sweet as a wasp," sighed Sanjeev, and they both laughed.

"You'd be lost without her."

"True."

He named the price.

It was a penny more than the week before - the offer was over.

Fear hit Jo like a punch, and the weight of life dragged her face and shoulders down.

She put what she had on the counter and whispered, "Can I owe you the penny?"

"Of course! Just forget it. It's OK!"

Jo could feel Sanjeev's embarrassment and pity like slaps on her hot cheeks. He had seen her bruises, when Simon had been careless.

"Thanks," she said, her voice husky, and she fled.

Her feet dragged on the way home. Simon would be there.

A red graffito caught her eye across the road. It was a space invader, a happy little thing. Jo remembered the game: rows of aliens moving down the screen, only to be shot and destroyed. Yet still they came, a crowd of them, and they always won in the end.

Jo found this strangely cheering, and again, in spite of everything, she smiled.

The space invader smiled back and waved a red arm, or perhaps tentacle.

There are decent people in the world - friends you haven't met yet.

The thought popped into her head as if the alien had spoken.

I ought to be frightened by what's happening to me, thought Jo. *But I'm only frightened with Simon.*

Jo saw Jack laughing at her husband, and the invader pushing him away inexorably, defending her.

Further along the wall was a stencilled image - a political thing of a man in a balaclava, holding a bunch of flowers.

"Hello," said Jo.

The figure bowed to her, and offered her the black ink flowers.

Suddenly Jo could smell honeysuckle, lilacs and roses. Oh, so long since she had smelled them.

She reached her front door.

The key turned in the lock.

Change is possible, thought Jo. She could feel a strength rising in her. *I am not as helpless as he thinks.* The possibility of colour and disobedience. She wouldn't mention the price increase. And Jo knew where Simon kept his secret stash of cash. Tomorrow, while Simon was at work, she'd get the locks changed and phone a solicitor.

She could do this.

Jack laughed. The invader jumped up and down with glee. The balaclava man danced. All along the wall, graffiti applauded her, a crowd of letters dancing, figures waving, faces cheering.

MERMAIDS DON'T DIE OF THIRST

It all made sense when I realised that I was a mermaid. Possibly an Antarctic one, given my build; my bulk would keep me alive in the bitter cold, and I would weave through the water, seal-graceful. But on land -

The man across the desk was talking at me. Not to me. At me. I can't understand most land-words. He said something about welfare and payments and jobs, and seemed angry with me, or he just hated me.

"I need money on land," I said, which was true, and that brought forth a new stream of words, even angrier than the words before. I had to do something, or be something, and get an up-to-date doctor's report. Prove that my legs would never heal.

There are no doctors in the sea. I would slide off the iceberg, after singing to the penguins, and swim, and eat and sleep. Or perhaps, if it got too cold, I'd visit the South Seas.

I'll be cold if I lose my home. I know that someone said something about that. A doctor's report. The doctor said all the land words too, very fast, and I was just sitting there trying not to cry. Tears are the closest I can get to the sea, you see. He said that I had to take my tablets, and that if I had heart pains I was to do something or other at once. I've explained to him several times that I can't remember to take my pills, and they don't seem to do whatever they ought to do anyway. He said that I had to make an effort. I can't remember what kind of effort or how I go about it, or what it looks like, so that I would know it if I saw it.

The angry man, telling me about welfare stopping, has now run out of words. He is waiting for me to leave, which is good because I don't feel comfortable or happy anywhere except the sea. Definitely not in offices.

The South Seas. You don't pay rent on coral. I wouldn't eat the fish. They're too beautiful for that. I'd eat the seaweeds, though they're beautiful too, but they grow back. It would be warm, and I'd probably lose weight. I'd tease the sharks, and dance with turtles, and clear up plastic, and eat seaweed, and drink seawater. Mermaids can. They don't have to watch their salt intake. In the sea, mermaids don't die of thirst. On land -

Outside the office I check my purse. I have eight coins. Spanish Doubloons from an old wreck. Pound coins from the bank. There will be no more after these are gone. I understand that much.

I will spend two of the coins now. It isn't the sea, but it's near enough to pretend. I pay and go in, and change into my swimsuit. It's blue-green and has lines like scales on it. It's the only item of clothing I've ever spent more than a tenner on. I get my goggles. I tie up my hair.

As I limp towards the pool, some children laugh at me in disgust. They can't believe that I'm so fat and so hairy. I haven't shaved my legs, or my bikini line, by which I mean the pubic hair that people might see at the edges of my swimsuit, for eight years now. In the ocean, mermaids' hair drifts with the water. All hair dances in the sea. It would be stupid to cut any off. The children's parents are trying to hide their laughter too, and for a moment I see through land-eyes: fat, ugly, hairy woman limping heavily. Wrong, all wrong.

It's only a flash, a horrible flash, and then I'm back. I limp to the deep end, which takes a while. The lifeguard recognises me, and we nod. She's the sailor who respects the mermaid. I am at the deep end. I curl my toes over the edge. I do that wonderful dramatic fall forward - and at just the right moment I push with my feet, and I'm a seal slipping off a rock and diving into the sea with hardly a splash.

I'm there. The only sounds are water sounds. Bubble, whoosh, bubble, whoosh, in rhythm as I swim. Swimming is easier than walking. Distant voices but they can't say anything to me. I pound up and down, and I can see the coral, such colours, and the azure of the water, and clown fish and angel fish. I can't get the odour of chlorine out of my head though. The old municipal pool has a strong smell.

Something special happens. I meet my manta ray, which doesn't happen often, and I'm on his back and he takes me through the sea and then up into the air and up into space, and we're swimming through the stars. You don't even need air or water if you swim through stars. They sing a music all their own. We glide down back into the warm ocean and we pass a family of turtles. I play with the babies. I say goodbye to my manta ray friend, and circle some seaweed fronds.

I am pounding up and down the pool, healing.

There is a pain in my heart, but it might just be sadness. Or healing.

I remember the doctor's words, but I can't deal with land-words now.

When the pain starts sparking in my arms and legs, I know that I am transforming. I am really becoming the mermaid that I am. I am pounding up and down, up and down, past the coral and the clown fish and the angel fish, and a whale is trying to warn me of something, but I laugh a rippling mermaid laugh. The pain in my heart is the scales forming. The pain in my legs, like shooting stars, is my tail growing.

The water is so warm. It's never this warm in a pool. I'm going home, home to the South Seas.

As my transformation is completed, my heart bursts into song.

WHAT THE SIRENS SANG TO ODYSSEUS

You have the biggest penis we've ever seen.
We have meat, but someone needs to light the barbecue.
We don't like intelligent, feminist men.
We like muscly adventurers with beard,
tunic and sandals. Such a hot look.
You're so adventurous! Talk to us about yourself.
You'd be the only man here.
Who cares about your wife?
We're just begging for it.
We're all virgins.
We have beer.

SARAH L DIXON

I AM THE CURATOR OF THE LOST THINGS.

I polish the broken number plates,
rejected toasters,
handles without mugs
and mugs without handles.
I flatten the sweet wrappers,
stained-glass litter, valued here.

I take the bottles the sea played with
and then discarded
and sort it into shades.

I collect fallen leaves and branches
and give them a place to decay
where they drop
flake by flake
until their fine lined skeleton crumbles too.

I am the curator of Lost Things.
I have found my purpose.

FINDING THE QUIET

I have travelled here on a road
packed with many vehicles of distraction
A four-lane motorway,
always rush-hour.
Pulling me in,
telling me to increase speed.
Keep up with tail-lights
of those in front of me.

Here is a coach loaded with map apps
so I can follow each step,
ordnance survey my way.
While I miss the flash of a kingfisher,
the patient stance of a heron,
graffiti, chimneys, exchanged smiles.

And now, an HGV of Netflix series
A camper van stuffed with books,
Not ones I will particularly enjoy,
but ones good enough to engage me
then feel obliged to finish.

A mini steeped in social media tweets
and all kinds of alluring notification bleeps.
It is bright and loud and can't be ignored.

A land-rover talks to me in podcast voices,
Pretends to be my friend,
draws me into other people's drama.
It TED talks me about all the things I could do
if I wasn't watching TED talks.

I will return to the motorway.
It is necessary for work,
But I vow to the B roads
and viewing platforms
I will stop there.
I promise the weir long breakfast visits.

DANDELION GODDESS VISITS CHATHAM LIBRARY

He was a slump of a man.
His legs rebelled against
these sedentary tasks.
Shelving stories, binding books,
stamping and scanning titles.

His legs wanted to be walking, in his heart
he is pacing Medway miles.
He is on the ground
where the hidden river runs.

As he makes coffee
with inky milk
he stirs thoughts
of all the dandelion clocks
he has wished on.

He imagines them teaming up.
Crash! The door of his imagination bangs open
and the Dandelion Goddess
lifts him above the turnstile.
She carries him off
into the November dusk.

He will miss the quiet lost property.
It doesn't judge him.
Like the public do.
It doesn't punch and prod
and bite like they do.
It sits in drawers,
hangs on hooks.
It waits patiently
for its owner.

Watches with broken straps,
frayed scarves,
an engraved Parker Pen.

All waiting for a return.
Their hope of reconciliation
is carried through the door in a storm.
But the debris of dandelion clocks
means the lost objects
can each make a wish
for home.

ALETHA FIELDS
HYON

Found my long lost cousin, Hyon (pronounced "Hahn"). Haven't seen him since I was nine, yet I never let go of him in my heart, though I'm now 51. When we cousins got to visit each other (our fathers are brothers), we didn't play with toys. We talked. We were hyperintelligent children who happened to be in the same tribe. I learned to spell his name before my own and wrote a song about it to remember it until I could write.

Our childhood exploits concerned what was growing outside that we could pick and present as food gifts to our huge family and how we could appease his mother and her kinfolk whenever we found ourselves in trouble—and we always found ourselves in trouble. Wagon full of earth goodies, our 5- and 6-year-old selves did not know we'd just razed the neighbor's budding garden.

That same visit, we snuck and made a Jiffy cake while the adults were busy talking. I was in awe of Hyon's ability to climb the kitchen counter to get the cake mix. "Only moms know where cakes come from. Hyon is magic!" The penultimate moment was yet to come—Hyon knew how to turn on the oven!

It was our cousin custom to get in trouble together. Don't know how my aunt always caught us, but she did. Hyon was the mastermind of our shenanigans and I was thoroughly amazed at his thoughtfulness toward all the details. So much so, he suggested we rehearse our apologies ahead of time and my aunt, his mother, always had mercy on us because of me. To this day, she is the only one who had faith in my pleas of innocence. With my remedial Korean, I would humbly begin the please forgive us process while Hyon kept mysteriously quiet. Aunt Yun would point her finger at us, chastise us, pinch us with her toes, and pausssssssseeeeee... just looking at us. After she said 아이고, we knew the thunder was about to end. Once we proved ourselves remorseful, she'd forgive us just in time for us to plan our next scheme!

Two years later, I saw Hyon again right after his father, my beautiful Uncle Alonzo, had visited us in Alaska. My uncle was a superhero to me because he had once convinced me he could break a wooden spoon in half. I didn't believe him. He said, "I'll show you right now." He went into the kitchen, got a wooden spoon, and broke it straight in half! I knew about God back then, but surely this was His brother. When my aunt nearly whooped him for breaking her spoon, I had met God's sister.

It was a huge treat to see a relative in those Alaskan days. Military families understand the luxury of seeing your loved ones. I relished that time with Uncle Alonzo. He sat with my sister and me every morning as we ate our breakfast. I was shy about saying grace in front of him, but he would encourage me to go ahead and bless the food. He smiled at me often and I thought he was John Henry because he would sit me and my sister on one leg. I could not wait to get home from school to see him each day that week. Within a month of that visit, a heart attack permanently separated our uncle from us, from Hyon, from Aunt Yun.

We flew to Washington State for uncle's homegoing. Usually only separated by geography, something more separated me and Hyon this time. It was eerie and incomprehensible to us children. We had no words, no understanding, no context for what was going on. During this visit, when Aunt Yun would see me somewhere in the house, she would gently take my hand and bring me into a room of beautiful colors. Though my ear for spoken Korean was very much in tact (Aunt Yun's dear friend and her husband got stationed in Alaska, lived across from us, and 아줌마 raised us in the daytime), no words in either language suffice to speak of these events to this day. I knew it was sacred to be with the Korean women in that room. The 아줌마 wore beautiful hues of blue and moved quickly, quietly, and reverently throughout the house to carry out the mourning traditions.

Two years later, Hyon and I reunited when Daddy's orders returned us to the Lower 48. Our first stop was Washington. Uncle Alonzo was not there to break a spoon or to talk my mom into letting us have extra sweets. I kept looking for him to turn a particular corner out of the kitchen. In my mind to this day, I still wait for him at that corner.

This visit, though, Aunt Yun let me watch her prepare my favorite, 불고. She told me to open my mouth and I was introduced to my first taste of raw meat. Delicious! Hyon taught me to roller skate, to do bike tricks, and long division. I showed him how to flip his arms to make it look like fast motion. We told dirty jokes like "Trick or treat, smell my feet, give me something good to eat." Aunt Yun, still the only believer in my post-shenanigan innocence, bought me a Mickey Mouse ring at the PX (post exchange). I was terrified of the huge 75-cent price tag and attempted to talk her out of such an expensive gift. She gave me a nonverbal Korean warning to be quiet. I became the fanciest girl on the planet that day in 1978. Don't you remember?

I cried at leaving Hyon and my aunt at the end of that trip. It was big to leave. It is yet bigger to see Hyon's face again.   Nice to see you again, Cousin!

ON COOKING, BLACKNESS, AND PLANTATIONS

As the morning mist rolled down the West Virginia mountains a few feet from her back porch, Grandma produced identical pieces of potatoes in the palm of her small hand. Ten pounds each morning for breakfast, one by one, eagle-eye precision. One woman. 4'10", 110 lbs. Long, silky hair in a net. Mother of six boys, two girls, buried her oldest and her youngest.

I'd learned when I could have my grandmothers to myself for long periods. After breakfast when all the others went out to play, I'd sneak back into Grandma's kitchen and sit on the same stool Daddy sat on as a child. Grandma rolled out her buttery pie dough by hand with a hypnotic rhythm. The apples cut to perfection. No recipe. Just hands, mind, heart. And an apple pie that would leave you dizzy at the first bite. Often she'd fluidly recite lines from James Weldon Johnson and other Black poets. She'd talk about her love of God, the hard labor assigned to Black folx—and, therefore, her body—and the pride she had in her children. Other times she'd tell me stories about how the white lady she once worked for encouraged Grandma to pass for white and if she did, the white lady offered to pay her college fees—if only Grandma wouldn't marry Welton. "Grandma, did you regret not going to college?" "No, indeed, honey. I love your grandfather." There was no trading miscut potato and apple pieces for dreams of "advancement." Grandmother Hazel is now 99 and still cooks for herself each day.

My grandmother in Kentucky, Helen, who is 93 and who may or may not choose to cook nowadays, would also rise early in the mornings to cook for our family. I'd sit on the stool next to her as she peeled fresh tomatoes with a serrated knife. Peels so thin, you could see through them. Granny cut around any bad spots in the tomatoes and then sliced them in flawless circles. She'd crack fresh chicken eggs into a bowl and I awaited the double yokes. Meant good luck. Every third Sunday in August, Granny fixed her flour batter for the chickens she and Granddaddy had cleaned. She'd fry the chicken to a mouthwatering brown, pile it high on a single platter to cool, then pack it up after breakfast to carry to the homecoming. Granny fried in three skillets at a time. How do you stack three skillets of chicken on one platter? Her geometry was impeccable.

Nowadays, my friends pine over my cooking. A few friends decided I was worth marrying over my salmon croquettes. Several lady friends offered me their lovin' in exchange for my peach compote and pistachio rosewater syrup. All said they'd pay to eat my food, so I boldly went into my friends' restaurant Spring Break 2003, toward the end of my fourth year teaching, and told them they needed some help. It was time to take my culinary prowess to the next level. That Tuesday I began and though I'd offered to work for free in exchange for the finer details of becoming a professional chef, Friday I walked out with a check and was told I didn't need to go to culinary school. Two months later I became the head chef inside the city's only all-Black, all gay kitchen.

I branched out into personal chef services after a year in the restaurant. Personal chef services was a study in plantation culture. I launched my business right around Derby. I detest the antebellum vibe of Louisville in general, but Derby hosts the plantation throwback party of a lifetime— every year. In my early 30s, I thought, "I bet one thing—some white people still want Black people cooking for them." And I was right. My first Derby as a personal chef was smooth. I gained several contracts. At the same time, I learned just how many plantation fantasies are alive and well in Louisville.

In front of his cigar-smoking and bourbon-drinking friends, a client referred to me as his family's cook: "That gal cooks for us." Gal? Gal who? Gal what? Their laughter cut short when I curtly said, "I'm not anybody's 'gal' and I'm not a cook. I'm a chef." I walked back to the kitchen and decided not to "Celie" the lemonade I'd just made. The next morning, as I finalized preparations for the Oaks brunch I was handling for his family and friends that day, the client came into the kitchen. His fingertips firmly on the edge of the counter, between his teeth he quietly said, "I don't know what your response was about yesterday, but if you ever do it again, you're fired." My heart began to beat hard enough to hear in my ears. African drums louder and louder. My great great grandmother's heartbeat. The fugitive's foot race. The yapping dogs. The field song's rhythm. In that moment, I embodied every Black chef on every plantation in every slave owner's kitchen. I took a breath from the bottom of my lungs. I wiped my hands, untied my apron, removed my cap, grabbed my knife pouch, popped a strawberry in my mouth, and walked out.

As I put my things in my car, his wife ran down and screamed, "Aletha, where are you going?! My brunch is in two hours!" I said, "You're right and Derby's tomorrow. Good luck!" Her husband left several threats on my phone: if I didn't bring my "Black ass" back to that house and finish cooking, he'd see to it that I'd never work another day as a chef in Louisville.

Honey, I laughed all the way to the bank. He'd already paid me. You can't afford my dignity. I am still cooking when I want and for whom I choose. Bon appetit and Happy Derby!

THEY STILL DO IT

Thirty-one years later,
They still do it
We used to walk, so in love
In the mall, holding hands
Actively irritating white folks
A white boy and a black girl, so in love
Actively irritating the standard
Milton and Rodney did it first
Two men
One black, one white
Irritating white folks
The nerve of being interracial
In front of folks
The absolute gasp of their nerve
To also be gay while at it
All these abominations
They're still at it

So at the airport
After 31 years
His arm secured my waist
My arm his
As we laughed, stopped and looked at each other
He kissed my cheek
I notice the stares
The mean mugs
The discomfort of the audience
Like any white folks who are right now irritated
I leaned up to his ear
The one I used to whisper my secrets into
I says, I says, "They still do it"
His arm pulled me closer
He says, he says, "So do we. Let them be sick"

JOLIVIA GASTON

NOT OUR CHOICE

Those whose lighter skin
Have privileged white
Darker blacks don't blend in
Their victimised
Venom tongues spawn
Who's to say we are not alike
To judge our skin day or night

Keep Segregation the white man wants
Let's fight trained to hate each other
By shades of colour
By occupation
The Master
They've chosen our names

Nigger
Blackie
Half breed
Mongrel
A bag of sweets
Bitter taste, to spit out
Disregard us
Left to rot

Racial words keep us apart
A merry-go-round
Which never stops
You're too dark
You're too light
No in between
All most white

Brothers, Sisters
African descendants
Take my hand
Walk with me

Across continents
Across oceans
Feel your feet on the ground

Our history embedded
Through Systemic racism
Colonialism, imperialism
Statues crumbled
The people's banner

Read it

Black Lives Matter
The UK is not INNOCENT

SEEDS OF MALICE

White cloak covers blackness in blue America
Marching boots golden badge
Your fate in their hands

Lucifer's personal selection
Infiltrated police department
Disguised in human form

AMERICA

Land of the free home of the brave
Cries out in labour pains
Devoured the richness of humanity

Spreads it's legs in the crucifixion
Of black men, black women, their children
The world watched and shouted:

'Black Lives Matter.'

BABY

Hush, hush sweet black child of mine
This newness cradled secure
Suckled on nipples
His gaze intentionally matched mine
This tiny human made from love
Black ivory worth millions

ELIZABETH GIBSON

WHY I USUALLY LIKE BEING QUEER

I like looking to people and feeling a gentle…*something*.
With many in my life, this is a solid stretch of yellow,
a public octopus whose tentacles we pat absent-mindedly
each time we meet, recognised as rain and cups of tea.

With people who may be a bit like me, it is a quiet thing,
maybe coy or cocky, an inside joke, a nervous question.
It is a cord inviting me, fairy hair from a childhood tree,
fragile and occasional, catching the firelight and nodding.

It is a rustle of feathers tapping on the small of my back
or a series of tiny ripples from invisible frogs. It is a voice,
an arm touch, subtlety and trust, coded flashes, symbols,
movement and breath, dots and colour. It is allowing time.

It is playing a long game. It is that final hug or high five,
the smile, the reassurance. You can grow old and be like us.
You can run a business and be like us. You can have kids
or cats or a caravan. You can live with your head held high.

CÉLINE AT CANNES

To openly gay filmmaker Céline Sciamma, who wrote and directed Portrait of a Lady on Fire

I keep that one scene ready, for when I need fire,
you there in your dark blazer, white shirt and collar,
gold feminist pin, hand on chest. The row behind
you are also elegantly dressed and as one, they rise
to revere you. It is an oil painting, faces in half-light,
red lips, hands blurred from singing out your praises,
lost for words. You pivot, drink it in, the auditorium
looking to you in this one, this ten-minute long take,
this piece of art, the making of history. Your gaze.
You say you have nothing to say, the film said it all,
you hug, you grin, you wink, you flirt with the tears.
Then, you blink hard, lead a line of stars, all women,
through the doors to take your place on the Cannes steps,
a supernova of rapture and respect blazing after you.

FEED

I want to know your stars with my eyes closed,
tongue guided by your jet trails and red flickers.
Show me the secret knock, the keys to the piano,
feed me sugar, heated sugar, caramel, saffron,
the second taste of our day, what we drank and ate.
I want to hear sounds like the Northern Lights,
that I didn't know I could make someone make.
I want to feel like a waterfall of ferns and fungi,
not having to do anything but feed the horse
who chooses to feed, strains her rope to never
have to stop, hooves clogging and stumbling.
I want dots of neon light sliding across my walls
until the bin lorry bleeps like a rainy alarm clock
and the cars whir like waves and we reluctantly rise.

MO HARROP

DONALD THE DANGEROUS

Donald the dangerous packed his trunk and made his way to the Whitehouse
Off he went with a Trumpety Trump
Trump Trump Trump
Spouting hypocrisy day after day
Migrant workers on minimum pay
Built him his towers wielding his powers
Now they are told they can't stay
I find it very scary that he has come so far
Going along with his venomous tongue
In his bulletproof car
Donald the dangerous world watch out
With him in the Whitehouse then I have no doubt
There'll be a world war and martial law
Then there'll never be any way out!

IN MY IMAGINATION

I've travelled the world
Been to the Pyramids and met the young king
Had tea with Caruso and together we'd sing
I've swaggered with Jagger
Met Bowie.. banned Towie
Saw Martin Luther King, and heard his great words
I've flown over Venice with beautiful birds
Saw Marilyn crying while gasping for breath
I've wept for the young and their untimely deaths
I screamed at Diana…DONT GET IN THE CAR..
I danced with Mandela and kissed both his hands
In my imagination, I've travelled such lands
Stood with terracotta soldiers and walked the great wall
Had breakfast at Tiffany's… Met Lauren Bacall
I've laughed til my sides split with Lucille Ball
I've rode with Hell's Angels at Daytona Beach
None of this is out of my reach
With tasselled leathers and long sequinned boots
Gone back centuries
Back to my roots
Told Bob Dylan he's looking quite rough
That he should really read MY stuff!
I've shown Andy Warhol my art.."This is mine"
He looked at me sideways and sipped on his wine
Wished Lennon had stayed in his room that day
Wished people with weapons would put them away
And parents that search for their children would find
At least some kind of peace of mind
I've kissed KD Lang…and I don't know why
Am I just living some kind of lie
With monied up maniacs rising sky high
A long way from here but still very near
With misguided supporters, cheering..they cheer
The people still mourning their battle scarred ancestors
It's still going on..the madness still festers
As bizarre and unreal as the old court jesters
Undeniable..unbelievable..unthinkable
I wish this was all in my imagination….

L. C. JANE

WHO CARES

These endless days
Empty, repetitive, wordless
Her body aches and groans
Like an old broken ship
Washed up on the rocks
Creaking bits ripped off
Bent and torn, worn away

Relentless pounding waves
Breaking the spirit
Whilst moored to the same spot
With a heavy chain

The blue and white paint
So bright years ago
Now peeled off giving way to
Decaying rot and rust
Years of anguish
Pain, grief, hopelessness

Another day; another dawn
Looking out of the window
Trying to find a reason
For being here
She waits
For a wave to carry her off
It never comes

TWO LIVES

A moment's glimpse
Snapshot of normal life
Laughing with friends
Summer dresses, bright flowers
Sharing of chocolates
Amusing tales and anecdotes
Human connection
Now your time is up

Home, a soft cell
Hiding behind closed curtains
Fear of what is to come that day
The inevitable abnormal
No one has a clue
Illness takes a hostage
She steps back into the darkness
And accepts her fate

ADY LAMB

KEYWORKER: COVID 19 ODE.

Front line worker,
Covering my mouth,
Gloving my hands and
Shielding my face.
Caring for your family,
Sister, aunts and mothers,
Grandma, Granddads and brothers.
Giving them my time,
Collecting their shopping –
Taking from the shelves another hero stacked.

Key worker,
Holding all the keys,
But entering no real doors,
Changing nothing but real lives,
His, theirs and yours.
Caring enough to risk it all,
Giving more hours than ever before,
All at minimum wage though,
Between £8.50 and £9 an hour no more.

Clap for us,
Send praise on social media,
But not holding banners with us in strikes
Or walking a mile in our shoes –
During these times it'll be boos.

And yet – send us out still
Pretend you know and have no hate,
Caring within our veins,
No matter our fate.

Call us what you will,
We don't do it to impress,
Just remember that there's key workers
Outside the NHS!

ELLIE ROSE MCKEE

LAST BEING FIRST

I can't believe I'm doing this.

I'm standing at the top of a cliff, ready to dive off into freezing cold water and I'm maybe more scared than I've ever been in my life. But she's beside me.

I turn to her, watch the wind whipping her hair back from her face, and shake my head. "I can't believe I'm doing this!"

She smiles at me so bright, it feels like something unlocks within my chest but, the next moment, I remember why that part's locked up in the first place and try and shove the door closed again.

Looking away from her, I jump.

The water feels colder than I even imagined, but only for a second. What follows is another second that seems paused – could really have been a year or a lifetime – and I'm numb. And I'm floating.

There's movement in the corner of my eye. I look and she's there again, floating right alongside. She takes my hand and pulls me towards the beach. I'm not sure I want to go. For a minute, I almost resist the pull of her. But, well, not being able to resist her had always been part of my problem.

On the shore, she's panting. I can't stop looking at her; at the way her clothes are tight across her body, weighing her down. The way her chest is heaving. She's looking back at me, smiling again, and I know more than ever before that I'm in too deep.

I can't do it. I turn away; fight her off when she grabs for my hand again.

Last night, I stayed at her house; her on the bottom bunk, me on the top. I asked her why her bedroom was done up like she was twelve and she said it had been decorated when she *was* twelve and they'd never really thought about changing it.

I don't know why, but I fixated on that. I guess it blew my mind that some things, for some people, hadn't changed in the past six years when everything seemed to have shifted for me.

Back when I was twelve, I was happy. I don't know when that changed – I'm not sure it was all at once – but now I can barely remember what it was like at all. I think I miss the certainty of it most.

"Laura," I said, biting my lip.

"*Kelsie*," she replied, mimicking my serious tone and then laughing.

The reaction almost made me back out of what I was going to say. I felt the words begin to dry out on my lips but, somehow, I took a breath and they floated out towards her.

"Laura, I… I think I'm going to kill myself."

She was silent. I waited. Then, when she still didn't make a sound – didn't laugh again or move or say anything I looked over the side of the bed to make sure she'd heard me and hadn't just fallen asleep or something.

She was looking back at me.

"You want to die?" she asked, finally, and it was almost like there was hurt in her eyes, but I'm not sure if I imagined that.

"No," I said after a long minute, my head suddenly starting to spin. "I don't want to die, I just…." My voice got real quiet. "I'm just not sure I know how to live."

"Oh," she said. She sat up.

After one more minute, I climbed down the ladder and sat beside her, our knees touching. When she opened her mouth again, I thought she was gonna yell at me or tell someone what I'd said. Panic rose in my throat as I wondered what they'd do with me if they knew – everyone else. My parents. Would they lock me away? Would they stop me? Did I want that? My head span so fast I thought I was going to throw up and I was torn between feeling surprise that I was feeling anything and worry at how ugly my vomit might make Laura if I puked on her sweater.

I was always worried about staining her, somehow.

She wasn't looking at me as she asked, "When?"

I blinked at her. "What?"

She turned her face so our eyes met. "When did you think about doing it?"

"Oh. I…." I had to look away from her. All of my words had gone missing. All of my reasons were right in front of me but it was like I couldn't reach for any of them when I had this one new, big question in front of me, too. And it was so small, as well. Four letters that would have made me hate her, if that were possible.

When. That had been what she asked. Not why. Not anything else.

"When?" I stammered. It was on the tip of my tongue to say 'I don't know,' but, in that instant, I made a decision. I looked back at her and said, "Tomorrow."

That was the first time she took my hand. She pulled me over to her tiny desk and didn't let go as she dug around in the drawers for a pen and notepad before eventually dragging me back to the bottom bunk.

"What's this for?" I asked, scared of the answer. Was she gonna get me to write a suicide note? Would that help?

"It's a list," she said. "What should be number one?"

I looked at her like I'd never seen her before; like I hadn't spent three years stealing glances at her, wondering if she could ever feel about me the same way I felt about her. I felt stupid. Then I felt angry. I wanted to rip the notepad out of her hands.

"Pros and cons," I spat. "Is that it?"

She rolled her eyes and smiled, putting me on the back foot; my anger back in my pocket. "No, silly. We should make a list of what to do."

"What to do?" I repeated. "What do you mean?"

I already had a plan for how to end it. I had several, actually. Should I tell her that? Would it matter? Suddenly, I found myself wanting to hear what *her* ideas were. I tossed out all of my own, wanting nothing more than for that conversation to last forever.

She was already busy scribbling when she said, "If you're gonna have one last day alive, you should make it good. What do you want to do?"

Again, I blinked at her. I opened my mouth but didn't know what to say.

"I think you should try base jumping," she said, carrying on in a casual, almost perky way as if she hadn't just blown my mind.

"You know the cliff overlooking the pier? It would be perfect for it. We could get the train into town and maybe grab an ice cream beforehand and go shopping after. You know, for warm clothes? I'll buy you a burger. There's a carnival in Red Rover, I think."

And on and on she babbled about all these plans for my 'perfect last day' and all I kept thinking was how cruel it was that she was making me fall even more in love with her even now. *Especially* now.

"So, you'll do it?" she asked, looking up at me from her list for the first time in maybe an hour, her eyes bright.

"You'll be with me?" I replied, not willing to commit myself to an answer until I had hers.

And she smiled at me like sun splitting the trees and I didn't know how to process any of it; how she could make my world feel okay and break my heart all at once. We'd have the perfect day and then it would just be… what? Over. All of it. Just like that? The thought resolved me. I knew then that it was the right call; that I couldn't go on when the sun went down and she walked away.

We fell asleep lying on the bottom bunk, my knees bent and pressed against the crook of hers; my arm around her waist, holding onto her like a life raft.

And now I'm looking out at the sea, drowning, and I can't let her hold my hand again knowing that if she takes it back, I won't be able to breathe and that she couldn't possibly hold on forever even if she wanted to.

I turn away. Her hand goes to my shoulder instead and I feel the heat of her skin, warm with adrenaline, through the wet cotton of my t-shirt.

"Come on," she says, and I follow like a bug transfixed on a fire, not really knowing myself or my actions. She sounds grave for the first time. For a minute, I think she's gonna tell me that she's the one that can't do it; that she's gonna give up and go home early, leaving me on the beach because she can't bear to stick around long enough for the sun to set.

I regret not letting her take my hand.

I'm looking at how many rings she has on, my eyes focusing on the flecks of glitter in her nail polish. The faint, faded lines on her knuckles where she tried to give herself a homemade tattoo, once, at the back of an unattended English class.

PEACE, she carved into one hand. *LOVE*, she wrote on the other. They were mostly healed up, the messages now little more than a ghost on her skin. I'm looking at them, forcing myself not to risk catching her eye and telling myself I won't cry in front of her if she goes now. I'm staring so intently at all the little lines on her hands that I don't notice at first when they get closer.

Her arms are around my neck and lips pressed against mine before my mind registers that she's moved and that she's no longer ahead of me but beside me; locked together with me. My lips move with hers all on their own and I can taste the salt from the sea on them. I don't know how long it lasts but, when we come up for air, I am breathless and panting and *alive*.

"Promise me," she says, looking so deep in my eyes I think she must know my whole life. Her fingers tighten around mine, the feel of her rings biting into the bone of my hands. "Promise me you'll still be here when I get back from holiday. Say you'll be here at Christmas, and Easter, and all the other breaks I get a chance to come back for."

I open my mouth and am just about to say that I will; that I'll promise her anything – *do* anything – but she shakes her head as if rethinking the request. My heart falls to the pit of my stomach and I think I feel the water I swallowed starting to come back up.

"Come with me," she says instead, looking nervous as if I was about to say no – as if I *could* say no. And I shake my head and smile at her and don't say anything because I don't know how to make the shape of words with my mouth while everything inside me is screaming; yelling that you can't save a person – not like that – and not caring that probably, someday, when she's at uni and I'm holding her back that we'll fall apart and I'll be right back here where I started. Alone.

"Come with me," she says again, the words a whisper on the wind. A plea.

And I do. I take her hand and go with her because how in the world could I ever say no, no matter that there's gonna be a when, not an if, in our future?

It sank in as we walked the rest of the way up the beach – that I had a future; that I *wanted* a future.

That this was the first day of the rest of my life.

WINGMAN

Lorna should have trusted her instincts and just stayed home. But Grey was always so persuasive, damn him.

"Come on," he'd said, "it'll be fun. A night out on the tiles is just what you need to forget about bitch-face."

For a second, Lorna had believed it might be possible. Grey had seized on her hesitation and now here she was, staring at the bathroom tiles of some fabulous club she couldn't remember the name of, regretting the whole thing.

With a groan, Lorna lifted her head from between her knees and stood up. She could do this. All it would take is stepping back into the thumping music and telling Grey she'd had enough. She could be back home and in her pyjamas in under an hour, if the traffic worked in her favour. But when was the last time anything worked in her favour?

She braced herself, opened the cubicle door, and narrowly missed colliding with a hot blonde who'd been, she assumed, looking for an empty stall.

"Shit!" they said in unison, before sharing a brief smile.

Lorna could have sworn there was a spark between them, but before she opened her mouth to ask for a name, let alone a number, the hot blonde blushed and ducked her head.

"If I could, um…." She gestured to the toilet door that Lorna was still blocking. "I mean, you're done, right?"

"Er, right," murmured Lorna, face flushing as she stepped out of her way. As soon as the door was closed, she considered banging her head against it. Because, *god! What kind of idiot am I? Making mooneyes at some chick just wanting to pee in private.* She shook her head, braced herself, and exited the bathroom back into the club proper.

Thankfully, it wasn't hard to find Grey. It never was. Wherever he happened to be, there was sure to be a crowd all around him. Sometimes an honest-to-god spotlight, too. Like he was the superstar he believed himself to be, or some random computer character with a side-quest.

Lorna was trying to figure out how to navigate her way through the crowd when Grey caught sight of her and made his way over, the crowd splitting for him like the Red sea.

"There you are!" He air-kissed her cheek. "Where have you been?"

"Hiding?" she hedged. "Making a tit of myself?"

"Oh, Lorn!" He squeezed her hand sympathetically and pouted. Actually pouted, as if he was a sixteen-year-old schoolgirl. "Not having fun?"

Lorna sighed, knowing she couldn't resist the pout, no matter how ridiculous it was. "I'm just not feeling it."

"But Lorn!" exclaimed Grey, batting his eyelashes, which were infuriatingly longer, and darker, and curlier than she could ever get hers. "I need you to be my wingman. There's this gorgeous blonde floating about who is to die for!"

Lorna frowned. "You want me to try and chat her up for you? Why?" God knows he didn't need the help. Was this just another pity thing to make her feel included?

"Please?" he said, batting his eyelashes again.

Bloody hell. "If I do this, will you please just let me go home?"

Grey opened his mouth – probably to talk her into not only doing what he wanted, but staying to watch *and* something else on the side, just because he could – when his eyes suddenly glittered.

Lorna turned to see what he was looking at and made eye contact with the blonde from the bathroom again.

"There she is!" said Grey, delighted.

Well, damn. "Fine, I'll go talk to her. But that's all, right?" Lorna moved off before he could answer. It was best to just get it over with.

An apology seemed as good of an opener as anything else, so she started there. "Uh, hi. I wanted to say sorry about before."

The blonde smiled and – *gah!* – it was dazzling. "Are you sorry for the weirdness or the almost concussion?"

Lorna bit her lip. "Uh, both, I guess? Anyway, I'm sorry. My name's Lorna, by the way."

The blonde put out her hand. "Shannon."

As inconspicuously as she could, which was probably as obvious as all hell, Lorna rubbed her sweaty palm on her jeans and shook the offered hand. "Nice to meet you, Shannon." It still felt as weird as before, standing there, trying to be cool while at the same time both trying to show a little interest and figure out if there was any interest going the other way.

To try and limit her mortification at least a little, Lorna shoved all her thoughts aside and just got on with it. Because it didn't matter that she was interested. Because A: she was a freak, B: she was on a mission, and C: Shannon was probably straight. The super cute ones always were.

"Listen, I know this is weird, but you see my friend over there?"

Shannon followed her gaze and nodded. "The life and soul of the party? Sure. What about him?"

"That's my friend Grey. He likes you, and it would be doing me a really big favour if you would go over and talk to him." Lorna was going to add a casual 'no pressure' at the end of her spiel, but Shannon had nodded again and was already off. *Typical.*

Lorna idled on edge of the dance floor, watching as Grey and Shannon laughed and whispered in each other's ears. She was wondering how long she should give it before she could officially consider herself off the clock and leave without feeling absentee best friend guilt. Then Shannon looked up at her and smiled again. Damn it all. She hoped to god Grey wasn't talking about her. He was always saying something, and it was rarely good. Like oh, for example, dragging her out tonight when he wasn't going to actually spend that much time with her.

Although she had to admit that, as Grey had promised, she hadn't thought about Ashton once. (Or bitch-face, as Grey liked to call her.) Maybe the night had been good for something after all.

Regardless, Lorna made her way to the bar at the same time she saw Grey heading there. She'd done what he'd asked and now she was definitely going home. She opened her mouth to tell him just that when he announced, "You are the worst wingman ever!"

Lorna reared back, offended, on top of everything else. "Excuse me?"

Grey shook his head. "You only sent me over a lesbian. But it's okay, because *she* is a good wingman." Grey leaned close and added in a whisper, "Shannon tells me the barman's been checking me out all night. I'm gonna go for it."

Lorna blinked at him. "Shannon's a lesbian?"

"Oh, totally," said Grey, complete with dismissive hand wave. "She's totally into you, by the way."

"She–? What?" No, that couldn't be right. Could it?

Grey gave her a little nudge. "Go on. She's waiting for you to talk to her again. Honestly, Lorn, do I have to do all the work?"

After another long look at her best friend to make sure he was serious, Lorna smiled and kissed him on the cheek. "Thank you, my darling Mr Wingman!"

ANNE MORGAN

MASKS

Colourful markets
From dawn till dusk
Changing in the Shadows
My Secret Life
No rules apply
This boyish attire
where people admire
My brusque walk
My cheeky ways
Freedom behind my mask
I feel more myself
Than myself can ever be

PAULINE OMOBOYE

A WOMAN'S RIGHT

WOMEN WANT JOY NOT PAIN

WOMEN WANT THE SUNSHINE AFTER THE RAIN

WOMEN WANT PEACE NOT WAR

WOMEN WANT LIFE WORTH LIVING FOR

WOMEN WANT HOPE NOT HATE

WOMEN WANT NOT HAVING TO WAIT

WOMEN WANT LAUGHTER AND HUGS

WOMEN WANT UNCONDITIONAL LOVE

WOMEN WANT THE COURAGE TO HEAL

WOMEN WANT THE SPIRITUAL FEEL

WOMEN WANT FIRST NOT LAST

WOMEN WANT SLOW NOT FAST

WOMEN WANT SHOPS AND SHOES

WOMEN WANT FIRST HAND NEWS

WOMEN WANT WHAT IS RIGHTFULLY THEIRS

WOMEN WANT WOMEN WHO CARE

WOMEN WANT TO LIVE LIFE TO THE FULL

WOMEN WANT BRIGHT NOT DULL

WOMEN WANT CHAMPAGNE AND CREAM

WOMEN WANT TO LIVE THE DREAM

WOMEN WANT!

WOMEN WANT

WOMEN WANT.

CUT AND DRY

Should I hand the towel in or leave it out to dry?

Dripping wet from life's ups and downs and stories passing by

Should I shake the creases out pretend there was never a fold?

Or leave it crumpled lying there sopping up the old

Do I sew the hem all straggled cut off the bits that fray?

Or do I buy a new one and leave the tag displayed

Do I fold it up quite neatly tuck in the sides now lame?

Or do I pat and rub the bits and hope that I might tame

I don't really want a shower that trickles just like rain

I need a bath where I can soak and ease all of the pain

Letting bubbles seep and tantalise seep into the pores

Close my eyes lay back and open many doors

If I ask so many questions there's obviously some doubt

Am I asking can I live with or can I cope without?

Do I want to look back on memories or haul in the nets so tight?

And grip with clasping fingers reaching in the night

If I ask so many questions does it mean I've reached the end?

Does it mean I'm sinking, drowning or just looking for a friend?

SARAH PRITCHARD

PRIDE KIDS

How many colours in your rainbow?
She asked. Six or seven? How many?
There are 6 if you are gay
There are seven if you are supporting the NHS.
He stared back at her face
With equally open enquiring eyes.
He took a deep breath.
If it's wings, it's gay of course
If it's an up side down smile it's NHS!
He said proudly.
They both laughed.
He added
I'm not sure if I'm gay yet or not
But I'm definitely an angel
My Mums say.

WHEN YOU COME OUT, YOUR WHOLE FAMILY COMES OUT WITH YOU.

When I came out
I was met by my mother's rolling eyes.
One by one she outted my whole family.
She started: I had a crush on another girl at school who was much better at cooking and hockey than me.
She was warming up: and I know your father fancied that younger Arab man when he was working away.
He'd giggle & smile whenever he mentioned him.
And I once caught your aunt drunk snogging another woman at a party.
Your uncle had to wade in and separate them. Too much sherry!
And into her flow she declared:
And even your Married-to-Mr Right-sister
Said she wouldn't say no to Nicole Kidman,
But it doesn't mean you have to do it all the time,
I mean where would it all end?
Her finale came later.
She proudly told me she'd come out to another Mother
Who'd told her about her son who was a drug addict.
Oh, I know how you feel, she declared
My daughter's a Lesbian.

UNLOCKDOWN

How do I unlock my new
Stepping back reflex from you
even though in my growing bubble
of permitted intimate huddle?

How do I find the key
to forget, relax or just be
Having been locked in so tight
My chapped fists are clenched in fight.

How do I let you in through my door
Act as if it's just as before
watch what you touch & hold
recapture my desire to enfold?

How do I begin again to reach you
Lay bare by your side on the beach you
taught me to think of to mindfully meet you
When I was already in lockdown long before.

JOEL SADLER-PUCKERING

FRIDAY 13TH

The devil masqueraded as a joker
and took them all for fools.
He shut down their communities
and bankrupted their schools.

He took them down a crooked road
and up a truly rotten path.
He stood back as they fought themselves
and hid a stifled laugh.

A dark, demonic blood sucker
with bad hair instead of fangs.
But it's a callous, hateful public
who now have blood upon their hands.

They voted for a homophobe,
a racist, cheat and liar.
So, welcome to your nightmare, dears
and the hell which will transpire.

DEAR ALAN
(For the statue of Alan Turing in Sackville Gardens)

There have been many times that we have whispered senseless diatribes into your ear, Alan.

When I broke up with my boyfriend, I opened a bottle of vodka at 11am - by midday, I was drunk and sat next to you on your bench in the park, telling you about all the outrageous things he'd said and done to me the night before. You listened patiently to my problems, didn't judge me and let me have a bite of your bronze fruit to feed my broken soul.

You told me to be logical and think it through.

At Manchester Pride, your fair-weather friends brought you flowers and took duck-faced selfies with you as they celebrated a freedom that you never had. I was outraged because don't think they knew who you were.

Because they don't know you like we know you, Alan.

They don't put you in clothes. They do not come and see you on winter nights when they are out on the town and they do not take photos with you wearing a flat cap stolen from a dear friend. They definitely didn't ever come and wish you a 'Happy New Year' and tell you to your face that they love you... and that's because they don't love you like we do, Alan.

When the government pardoned you for the crime of being 'a homosexual', you deserved the box of 'Miniature Heroes' we bought you. Although, we realize now that chocolate is not your thing and you would have preferred to just have another bite of your poisoned apple.

We could tell on that day, by the look on your face, that you didn't want a pardon (or the chocolates) if everyone else wasn't getting them too.

THE HUMANITARIAN AND THE FIRE EATER

Beach bar. Disco lights.

Thai fire eaters slave
over hot flames
to please groups of
Europeans clapping like seals.

I sat chill. Zombie. Watching.

Then she arrives -
and blocks my view.

Her T-Shirt reads:
'Humanitarian Affairs'.

She wears mass produced
slave labour trainers.

But I know the truth because
no true humanitarian
blocks your view
of fire eaters
dancing for tips.

PHIL TONGUE

NO BANANA SPLIT

From early love at first sight

For years trying as we might

Uphill struggle, managing through

Paying bills, our long-haul view

Together our gift, family blessed

Our house, home, our love nest

In the past, over and done

No winners, losers in the long run

Our vision, dream, a nightmare

Legal bills, no money to spare

Our lives changing, going our ways

Reflecting, this temporary phase

Stressful move, memories left behind

A new home, a mountain to climb

A bitter pill, amicable split

Now in shreds, your football kit

Divorce absolute, over, it's final

Whatever, I'm keeping the vinyl

TAKE IT IN YOUR STRIDE

There's no shadow, or a dark cloak

Carry with life, I'm a normal bloke

Daily routine to follow, it's no hardship

Medications help, taken with a sip

Always a first time, I crashed the car

Who needs to drive, family take me near or far

Crashing around, first time unaware

Thirty years since, now more care

Unpredictable times, hitting the floor

Even stuck behind the bathroom door

Maybe a shock, not the end of the world

A minor detail, epilepsy's a word

Be positive, no matter how you've cried

Always others worse, take it in your stride

LOUISE VEE

JUST SOME OF THE THINGS, I HAVE DISCOVERED, THAT CANNOT STOP YOU HAVING A(NOTHER) MISCARRIAGE:

Telling people you're pregnant. Not telling people you're pregnant. Hoping you'd used up all your bad luck when you lost two babies at once last time, because nobody can be that unlucky, can they? Spending thousands and thousands and thousands of pounds. Taking so many hormones, so many times a day, for so many weeks, that the pharmacist questions your dosing. No caffeine, no alcohol, no gluten. Paying £250 for someone to scratch your endometrium, and asking your mum if it can be your Christmas present. Missing the Christmas party because you just spent £75 on oestrogen patches. Taking twelve different vitamins a day. Learning how to run so you lose 10kg. Stopping running at embryo transfer so you don't dislodge the embryo. Thirty minutes of gentle walking per day to ensure blood flow to the embryo. Knowing how many cells your embryo has for the first five days of his development. Knowing he would be a he, because he was fast-cleaving by day three and fast embryos are more likely to be boys. Freezing him for six months so you needed less time off work. Crying down the phone at the embryologist who told you he had defrosted really well. Watching him with your own eyes beginning to hatch out of his shell after he was defrosted. Spending time cuddling other people's babies because hormones. Avoiding other people's babies because insanity. Paying £50 a session for acupuncture - for two years. Seeing a fertility counsellor free of charge for a year because last time nearly actually killed you. Being discharged from NHS PTSD counselling because you're "doing really well" managing your flashbacks to intensive care. Only eating warming foods so as not to divert energy from your womb. Wearing lucky socks with pineapples on because pineapples are a fertility food. Drinking organic pomegranate juice to grow your womb lining. Celebrating when your womb lining gets to 9mm. Eating brazil nuts to support implantation. Injecting yourself with hormones allegedly made from the piss of menopausal Italian nuns. Ditching most of your plastics for glass because BPA. Not using nail polish for two years because formaldehyde. No scented candles because fumes. Buying a fridge thermometer to check your drugs don't freeze. Buying a bath thermometer to check your embryo doesn't boil. Filtering all your water. Using three different mindfulness and meditation apps. Doing random acts of kindness to rebalance your root chakra. Obsessing over a site called Miscarriage Reassurer, that reassures you you have an 83% chance of a healthy baby. Not being reassured, because last time apparently had odds of 1:30,000 and that still happened. Buying many, many tests to see the lines getting stronger and then panic-buying more when they don't get as strong as they should be. Having blood tests at 48 hour intervals for two weeks, to see if it's ectopic again or just plain old failing. Spending whole days of your life scouring the internet for similar stories with happy endings and not finding them. Going to a different hospital for a second opinion. Talking to him and begging him to stay and be healthy. Praying to a god you don't believe in, just in case.

Pretending everything is absolutely fine, because it's the done thing and who wants to hear about this stuff.

Wishing he would have had the good sense to kill you properly, this time, instead of just tearing out your heart.

ANASTASIA VOROBYEVA

BECOMING BROKEN OPEN

This is how people live. What's the first thing a kid says when he learns how to talk? 'Hey, tell me a story'. That's how we understand who we are and where we come from, what we shall do or what we are doing, what would be my journey and how I will care or not about 'others'. Somehow we rarely hear the real story from mouth to mouth from those about whom we form our prejudice. We rather hear stories ABOUT them.
Or we don't at all.

I was born in Moscow when my mom was sixteen and my dad a bit older. They divorced when I was 3 years old and my grandma took charge of me. Every day I was looking at the window reflection in my room, which I was sharing with granny, trying to create pants from my skirt, holding a piece of dress in between my thighs, while Russia and America signed the declaration about ending the Cold War.
I loved to collect wooden sticks on a street, it brought me closer to Jacky Chan in my imagination. Oh my, I always loved him and how his body moved. At the age of ten when my country started a First Chechen war I had a friend, a blond boy with a shy smile and the same character. All summer time in our duet I was in charge of protection from other kids. It was new and dangerous but so exciting for my age; adventures and other fun stuff grown ups wouldn't like us to do. I was a Chuck Norris for sure in this friendship. Our main activity was stealing golf balls from a big field infront of my apartment block, then exchange one to another, green and white for a pink one with a stripes and orange on two white ones. We had quite a collection.
Once we got caught with the golf stuff and my friend was terrified as if we are spies and need immediately to take some poison to be sure they will not get the information. They said the girl can leave, pointing to me and the boy will work for a day on the golf court to collect balls as a way of punishment. I didn't get it. - Hey, I also stole your balls, I can stay as well - I said proudly. All that summer I was quite a badass with required courage for this world.

But like in most drama stories the summer time always comes to the end.

Suffering years started at school, all because I started to be somebody, but not myself. The need to be somebody always separates me from myself.

I didn't have a possibility to choose my clothes and anything else because I didn't even know I have a choice.
- Be a girl, stop climbing garages
- Iron your dress, what others would think about you?
- Look at Alice - she is always with a good manners.

These were narratives I was growing up with.

I remember myself standing in front of the class 8 years old and starring into the portrait of some famous biologist on the wall. I just liked his suit and funky haircut. Both of my sweating hands holding my skirt and I couldn't say a word in front of anyone. Why is that? Where is my inner Jacky Chan? Have I lost it with my dress? It felt so much like having someone else's skin. Although I'v got quite a few complements from my grandma about my look.

Next episode I remember is myself 26 years old, standing under the spot lights on a stage in front of the big audience of a black box. People applauding, I am holding flowers, smiling with my whole body and feeling myself like a fish in the sea saying some jokes in a microphone. It was my first production I was directing about Women in a Modern Society. The first and only words I got from my grandma afterwords "You look like a boy in these pants, they are terrible!" Well, it struck me hard, but at least I am free now in my own expression, I thought at that time. That's the miracle of how much a comfortable outfit was changing my inner world. I guess because even clothes are associated deeply inside with certain narratives about gender, sexuality, culture and much more human stuff.

Go back to my early ages, teenagerhood in 2000 came together with first terroristic attacks in Moscow, while NATO were bombing Yugoslavia and a young guy Vladimir Putin came into power.

I started to feel explosions in myself; a first shiney and slippery path into an unknown grown up world through my first kiss. Excitement growing from the lower belly up to my chest. Slow dance with Scorpions song "Time", if you can hear first words playing in your head now, you definitely got me! Stuffy diaper air, sweaty shirts and seductive eyes glimpse in a dim light. Desires to be kissed, to meet somebody not only for a dance. Already quite a few girls from my class said goodbye to the innocence of girlhood.

- Come on Nastya, you need to catch up on this marathon - I was pulling myself.

First, second, third kisses, it was quite special and my fire was up till the moment it was coming to the full experience. Yes, I didn't like boys at all in love matters. But again like with the clothes, I didn't have a choice. Everyone around me was enjoying it which made me feel like something was wrong with me and I kept it in secret, as well as I kept trying with the hope something will change in how I feel about it. But how could I know there were options? I didn't seen any, I never even knew something more than boy plus girl existed. My world was pretty small, I could easily pack it in my bag and hold onto it as the only right way to live.

My world crashed and expanded on my first Playback Theater World Conference in Frankfurt on which I knew only a few words in English. And now 10 years after I am writing my first book in this language. I would think you are crazy if somebody would tell it to me that time. The new chapter, but I would even say completely different book of my life started in 2011. While I stand at the beginning, the world was saying good bye to Muammar Gaddafi, Bin Laden, son of nation - Kim Chen Ir and closing the last page with the end of the Fidel Castro era.

Unknown before in its geometry façades and the narrow streets and passages that run through the new districts were taking my breath in this big city of Germany. Smells of Christmas markets burst into my lungs with a light nausea. I found myself in a hall of hundreds of people, speaking words which for my ears was like melodies, chords, basses, percussions or little bells with all gradation of sounds. May be it's good I have no idea of the meaning, it brought me benefits of enjoying something beyond words. That was the melody of the world. Some voices we hear louder and some we barely recognise, a perfect and unfortunate reflection of humanity. The world became an infinite galaxy in that room for me. How could I learn this music of the world? It scares me and brought excitement at the same time. But my life changed. People I'v met gave me the possibility to see myself and helped me to stop that marathon of trying to fit into someone else's ideas about myself. I broke through and started my journey of exploring a bigger world with all its complexity.

What's the first thing a kid says when he learns how to talk? 'Hey, tell me a story'. That's how we understand who we are. What would be my journey? Stories I was surrounded by didn't have any narratives about gay people, so I tried to fit in with what I knew was right.

But with all my heart I could say that now my story helped me to be broken open, to listen deeply and be more sensitive for the stories of others.

How can I not be myself, everybody else is already taken! Dr Seuss - I whisper in that busy hall.

Since that time I ask myself if my country has shifted under my feet, or did it stand still while I stomped along my road toward whatever I'm chasing to discover.

BECOMING A REBEL

The art has made the activism more creative and bold, the activism has made the art more sharply focused, more grounded, more dangerous.

I opened the door and thick air with a smoke of cigarettes and gin & tonic tickled my nose. A small wooden stage with a spot light; tattoos on the hands of poets reaching the microphone faster than a word; musicians with all kinds of haircuts; stand-up comedians straighten hair with a confident gesture; drag queens with bright feathers and golden pendants laying on the massive feminine chests and all kinds of other people, no one style repeated. Paradise of diversity celebration and pleasure of being yourself when you are not overwhelmed with the thoughts about what others are thinking of you, or where is safe and where to hide.

It was 2013 outside and I just started my journey exploring my real self and calling the rainbow flag of my home community, getting my first impression and it comes with a shock as a full package in my country. The same year for the purpose of protecting children from information advocating for a denial of Traditional Family Values Russia puts out an anti-gay law and provoked lots of aggression towards this community. As if standing by the person with a long neck - yours might also grow. As a way of protest and immediate action I start doing Playback Theater with this community. We had a group once a week, a safe space to share stories and be free in spontaneity. My dream to create a Queer Playback group was amputated that night I opened the door of the club.

It was a Coming Out Day. The day of celebrating sexuality and raising awareness around that topic. People chatting, dancing, taking turns to come up on stage with a song, poetry and all kinds of performing arts. Wrinkles getting deeper on faces from the smiles and you can't rest your muscles. I am waiting my turn by the bar sipping Margarita, feeling tipsy from the liberation of my mind. That kind of liberation when you don't think before holding the hand of your lover in public or catching an angry look from strangers in the subway because of your haircut. You never think of safety if you already have it. That is called privilege. You can not choose the moment when oppression will touch you, it is choosing you.

I am waiting to step into the spot light and share information about my Playback group for the community. To say everyone is welcome to join our safe space of stories. The moment I am making a step with a microphone - the world stops. Like in a blockbuster movies slow motion scene coming up on the screens.

Around 20 people with black ski masks over their faces are entering our small space. While one of them raises a hand with a gun - others turn tables over, beating some unlucky folks on the floor. Sounds of breaking glass and scared people, homophobic statements are crashing my ribs. My brain couldn't believe it's happening for real. I found myself sitting in the corner covering my head and still holding a mic in my hand, as if I am a news reporter at war with the small unfolding infant of me but I couldn't do anything.

Next scene is exactly what you see after the battle. Dusty air seen very well under the spot lights, a crunch of broken bottles, glasses and human souls mixed up with blood as if someone had spilled paint on that grey canvas. Pretty surreal and quick transition from the original spirit of freedom and celebration of the space. People are shocked and frustrated. Police sirens somewhere in the background.

But the most painful and devastating was what happened after. Police checked the place and said into our faces: Hey I hope you understand that we are not going to open investigation, nobody wants to be in trouble with people like you.

Explosion of anger and misunderstanding, how somebody can say it to human beings because they are different, had been coming up slowly and stuck in my throat, I barely can exhale anymore.

Days after I saw in the news people protesting against the development of a new business center in the forest zone, healthcare problems, a few criminals getting caught by the police and new promises of the prime minister to move towards democracy. Nothing about what happened that night.

I am supposed to catch a flight to NY a week after what happened and spend a few days with good friends of mine. Instead of a few days - I spend a few months postponing my tickets. Suffering from inflamed brain by making a decision which could change my life forever. Stay safe in a foreign country and not be able to come back for 5 years to see my friends and family or come back without knowing if I can be somebody for my beloved country or being an error on the desktop. A very uncomfortable spot to be which takes all liquid out of the body till the last drop of a tear. I made a decision to return to Moscow. To come back in order to become somebody and change the narratives. To find out who are these people who can't speak because of the social pressure. If we want to change the world by storytelling, we need to change power structure for the storytellers.

And I will come back someday but not by my weakest part, but by my strength - I whispered to myself looking at the Liberty statue becoming smaller and smaller throughout the window until it disappeared.

I was cut in half like in Cyprus, like Berlin, like Korea, like all the other places in a world that was no longer one thing or another.

That is how I choose my path to be broken open and become a peaceful warrior. There is no broken heart. It's a heart we break open to see wider and dig deeper into empathy we need more than ever

STEVEN WALING

CREPUSCULE WITH NICA

The weight of his intelligence   in late
American twilight   stands awkward in fur coat

and hat   white gloves   Here she's with
some of her three hundred cats   Order

out of chaos   Monk's fingers jumping chords
needs someone to look after him   Her

blue Bentley by the kerb   "The most
beautiful man I ever saw"   Three wishes:

To be an excellent musician   Long shadows
of the post-war blues   her leopardskin

blowing in the breeze   They called her
the Jazz Baroness   mother to a tribe

of cats who sleep all day and
play all night   *To have a crazy*

friend like you   whose namesake's a moth
once raced Miles Davis down Fifth Avenue

her impulse to collect   paintings   musicians   cats
first time hearing Round Midnight   That time

cops took his licence   Nica took his
rap   I heard that junkie Parker died

in her apartment   "I should care   I
should go without sleeping"   Monk prowling round

the melody   Dark clubs where the cats
create havoc in the instruments   new sounds

create themselves at night   and she's home
in the halfdark streets   *A happy family*

Nica says   "Thelonius   you have that already

INTO THE WOODS

under our feet   What's scrabbling thru the
undergrowth   Roar of the motorway   Rattle
of a tram   squirrels carry fairy tales

in tiny hands   What was this place
kiss-chasing thru remnants   of ancient woods
not large enough to sustain   Kids

BMX over bumps   Someone said it was
a girls' school   nuns teaching tennis or
netball on a sunny afternoon   old

trees new growth   next to the river
bursting banks   clearly we were lost
at regular intervals   among ecosystems

built on reclaimed land   birdsnests   Then
for a while an all-weather pitch   sports
club that sort of thing   Cars thunder

over the overpass   bisecting the wild
creation of wetland   but we're never
really lost   as trees take over the old

changing rooms   wild ramsons   bluebell
ducks under shelter and a cormorant
batwinging   by the lakeside path   fish

avoid the hooks in clear water
90 foot deep in places   teal   snipe
apparently   and at least 3 heron   Boughs

hung with words   by the footpath dreams
of happy trees   sad trees   fallen trees
this the kind of place   you'd likely find

a ring or   an old sword   rising
from the lake or   by the boatyards perhaps
where the old girls play   in flooded courts

THE KIRKYARD CAT
(St Bride's Church, Lochranza)

Beautiful island is this
on which floats the moral
point the remains of

unknown woman and child
hail gust we know not
peace to you till

day dawn the ginger
cat seeks shade among stones
true spot of tranquillity

lets us stroke its
fur the shadows flee away
sometimes the simplest space

is most sublime the
church an upturned prow graves
fallen over drowned at

continuous line of ministers
since medieval wherever you go
you're always here more

things learnt in woods
than from books a quiet
Englishman who so loved

life did not matter
what the weather beloved husband
wonderful wife see you

soon always this island
the undersong of silence though
you are absent you

are near from grandads
to teenagers 4 dead children
one family who survived

in the rose window
ship full sail the blessing
of loaves and fishes

very clean & well equipped

CARSON WOLFE

BUTCHES CAN'T WEAR SKIRTS

Butches can't wear skirts,
the admins of the Butch Fashion Club say.
Skirts are less valid? Less masculine? Less gay?
We've come a long way
since the 'three piece rule'
Where cops arrested butches for looking too cool.

"I have a baby pink sock under each black boot.
And my wife's lace panties, the pocket square of my suit.
Three articles of femme I think you will find,
so uncuff me Mr Officer if you'll be so kind".

Gender bending was outlawed, cross-dressing a crime,
you had to conform to your gender roll of the time
Otherwise they'd beat you and rape and abuse,
I read all about it in Stone Butch Blues.

The skirt once oppressed us, so we flipped the law,
It was illegal to wear trousers and we wanted more.
Elizabeth Smith Miller, she started the fight.
A suffragette in trousers, it earned us the right.
But this led to a contentment for anything deemed *femme,*
whilst simultaneously taking sex from them.
Sounds a lot like toxic masculinity
If you ask me.
So
are we
really
actually
free?

Because the skirt is the second oldest garment worldwide,
they are the fabric of many cultures and people wear them with pride,
they've been worn by all genders for thousands of years,
but now men in anything *femme* will summon some fears.

Dear Butch Fashion Club
Realise
That it's your masculinity we need to decolonise.

Because Muslim men in Saudi wear Thobes,
and then there's:
The Kilt, the Dhoti, Fustanella and Sulu.
The Tunic, the Gho, Gallibaya and Paschou.
The Kikoy, the Kaftan, Kurt Cobain in a dress.

But butches can't wear skirts, what a mess.

Fijian men must wear skirts on a Sunday they are told,
If they dare to wear trousers it is god who will scold.
The Western skirt was really put to the test,
when on stage appeared, Vin Diesel, P.Diddy and Kanye West.

If they can do it then why can't we?
They 're all as manly as manly can be.

The problem is in the labels that we fold ourselves into,
but these are the only communities that we can turn to.
It's a Butch/Femme/Macho/Lipstick/Stud origami.
And whilst I have the opportunity, write better women Murakami!

These identities imprison and act on us without consent.
It's on us to act with them in a way to reinvent,
the ideals of masculinity that have caged us in
This I reckon… is where we can begin.

MANTZ YORKE

A GRADUATE'S LAMENT

My college degree was sold as a dream,
but its total cost I never foresaw:
I'm burdened with debts I'll never redeem.

Graduates are losing employers' esteem
and mid-level jobs are no sinecure.
My college degree was sold as a dream.

A degree, they said, would make us the cream
that floats to the top – but cream's turning sour:
I'm burdened with debts I'll never redeem.

Robots now function to programmed routines,
left to get on with them, hour after hour.
My college degree was sold as a dream.

My work is due to be done by machine:
since automation is sure to endure,
I'm burdened with debts I'll never redeem.

The job market's thin; it makes me blaspheme.
The story they told? A caricature.
My college degree was sold as a dream:
I'm burdened with debts I'll never redeem.

TRICKLE-DOWN ECONOMICS

The hospital is in crisis:
its doctors are overworked,
the deficit's getting worse,
and the vacancies for nurses
are higher than was planned.
Agencies fill the nursing gaps –
but at a cost that, very soon,
the budget won't withstand.

Patients are unaware
the dishes on the tallest block
are sending and receiving
microwaves of cash
between investment houses
as financiers seek profits
to stuff offshore wallets
already over-stashed.

A rental accrues, of course,
from the paraboloid dishes'
prime positioning –
but it's the tiniest trickle
from the billions sent zinging
by dealers' algorithms
day in, day out, above
decaying, cash-strapped wards.

BIOGRAPHIES

Rebecca Audra Smith

Rebecca writes queer intimate poetry exploring the domestic terrain of love and lust. She is currently running the workshop Trans Writes and Free Writes with performance artist, DJ and activist, Jess Rose. Find her poetry in Lustful Feminist Killjoys, co-atuhored with Anna Percy, published by Flapjack Press.

Ruth Broome

Ruth is currently teaching art at an International School in Chengdu, China. Born in Greater Manchester she went to drama school in Birmingham in the 1980's and moved to London. She returned to the North West in the 90's and received a fine art degree from Liverpool John Moore's in 2000; trained in Transactional Analysis and completed a master's in Social Science from Edge Hill University in 2019. She is currently reading my new poetry and prose at the famous Spittoon in Chengdu and have recently read as part of the International Civic Poetry Party, Crane Woods.

Cathy Bryant

Cathy Bryant's poetry collections are: Contains Strong Language and Scenes of a Sexual Nature (Puppywolf, 2010), Look at All the Women (Mother's Milk, 2014), and Erratics (Arachne, 2018). Formerly homeless. Cathy is disabled, bisexual and neurodivergent. She runs the 'Comps and Calls' website of opportunities for impoverished writers at:

www.compsandcalls.com/wp

Sarah L Dixon (www.thequietcompere.co.uk)

Sarah L Dixon is based in Huddersfield. She had recent acceptances for Bloody Amazing and Mancunian Ways. Her books are 'The sky is cracked' (Half Moon Press, 2017) and 'Adding wax patterns to Wednesday' (Three Drops Press, 2018). Sarah's inspiration comes from ale, being by/in water and adventures with her son, Frank (10).

Aletha Fields

Aletha is a queer African and Indigenous American poet who lives in Louisville, Kentucky,USA. For over two decades, Fields has written and performed her poetry across the United States. She was honoured to meet and perform alongside one of her favourite poets, African American Last Poet Dahveed Ben-Israel (David Nelson).

Currently and in conjunction with the Louisville Story Program, Fields is co-authoring a book on the effects of mass incarceration on five Louisville families, including her own. The book will incorporate Field's poetry and prose. She will also serve as editor-in-chief of the final project. Fields, 51,is the mother of two adult children and is married.

Jolivia Gaston

On her poem, 'Not Our Choice': 'I was so angry at the death of George Floyd so I decided to search my mind for what Black Lives Matter means to me. In the early years of my youth, I heard these racial names it was accepted as the norm. Looking deeply into Blue America, I saw raw systemic racism in the police departments. Finally, I wanted to show the love a mother holds for her black child.'

Elizabeth Gibson

Elizabeth writes poetry and fiction inspired by nature, travel, body image and identity, as well as her experiences within the wonderful creative women's and LGBTQ+ communities in Manchester. Her work has been published in journals including Confingo, Popshot, Litro and Strix, and she has two poems in the Mancunian Ways anthology from Fly on the Wall Press. She won a Northern Writers' Award in 2017 and was shortlisted for the Poetry Business' New Poets Prize in 2018. She has performed at the LGBT Foundation, Manchester Literature Festival, The Poetry Café, and Walk for Women, for International Women's Day.

Mo Harrop

Mo has loved poetry for as long as she can remember. As a child, she would make up little poems, and at school she would make my friends laugh with comedy rhymes. Here she tells us about her journey into poetry: "It was just something I did and never really thought about. As an adult, I would jot down a few words but never did anything with them. Approximately four years ago I looked up some open mic' poetry meetings, one of which was the Write Out Loud group at Sale Arts Theatre. It was here that I read out some of my written work and gained confidence in doing so.'

L.C. Jane

L. C Jane has been a carer for 15 years, looking after a daughter who has severe mental health issues. She explains her journey to poetry here: 'It is a very hard and lonely path. I have never written poetry before, so this is very experimental. I was inspired to start by a close friend who is a poet. I am discovering it is a great way to express feelings and emotions that are difficult to verbalise. It gives me a sense of freedom, creativity and expression amid the lockdown of the current CCOVID-19 pandemic.'

Ady Lamb

Ady is a creative and ambitious person from the North West, who is hoping to train as a Teacher of English next academic year. She has spent much of my life retraining in order to achieve my goals. She is very determined and driven; one of her goals also includes one day hopefully to have an anthology all of her own! Her day job consists of being a Keyworker supporting people with critical care needs and devoting the rest of my time to my family! She likes reading and joins in on my local virtual spoken word night every month with Testify Poetry.

Ellie Rose McKee

Ellie is a writer from Northern Ireland. She has had poems published by Arlen House, Nine Muses Poetry, and Poetry NI; has had short stories included in Women Aloud NI's 'North Star' anthology, The Bramley, and The Bangor Literary Journal; and has been blogging for over ten years.

Ellie Rose McKee is a writer from Northern Ireland. She has had poems published by Arlen House, Nine Muses Poetry, and Poetry NI; has had short stories included in Women Aloud NI's 'North Star' anthology, The Bramley, and The Bangor Literary Journal; and has been blogging for over ten years.

Ann Morgan

Professional procrastinator… Coffee snob… Actor in diversity… Herstoryteller… Relax Rebel… Slayer of shame… Catwoman-in-disguise

Pauline Omoboye

She discovered her desire for the spoken and written word at a early age and went on to hone her skills through several experiences including a writers group with Lemn Sissay and women only writing groups including Nailah (which means 'one who succeeds')

She is a published poet who has a book of poetry: 'Purple Mother'. Her work is published in many anthologies including one called 'Hair', which looks at the journey into African and Asian experience of hair through poems, stories and hair tips.

Sarah Pritchard

Pippi Longstocking like free ranges with dog kids Rufus & Georgia lurchers 'turnupstuffing' in the wild. Still personal & political & passionate about poetry strolls & poetry en plein air.
Published in many anthologies from Beyond Paradise, Crocus 1990 to the most recent Mancunian Ways, Fly On The Wall & The People's Republic of Mancunia, Flapjack Press 2020.

'After The Flood' (a stormy swim through the 1953 floods of East Anglia) was finalist in Local Gems' 2017 NaPoWriMo chap book - 30 poems in 30 days. Her 2nd collection 'When Women Fly' came out in 2019 published by Hidden Voice Publishing.

Co-editor of Hidden Voice Publishing anthology 1 & 2.
Fb: Englishalien
Email: sarah60pegasus@gmail.com

Joel Sadler-Puckering

Joel Sadler-Puckering is a Mancunian politically minded poet. His debut collection 'I Know Why The Gay Man Dances' was released on Kindle and paperback in April 2017 and was a best seller on the LGBT poetry chart. His follow up collection 'Feral Animals' was also a best seller on the same chart. He is co-editor of Hidden Voice Publishing Anthologies (Volume 1 & 2).

His poems will take you on both a personal and political journey to explore the many ways that we, as human beings, might find our freedom compromised in modern life.

Phil Tongue

Phil found poetry with the help of a good friend when they took on the Napowrimo challenge in 2017. Ever since, he has written a poem a day for his blog: 'unclephilsblog'. His passion is Northern Soul music which he has enjoyed since the 70's and he loves to bake posting under the name of #unclephilsbakery.

He has won a local competition within our libraries with the topic 'Our area', was on radio Torbay reading one of his poems and has two poems that were published by New Mills Arts Festival.

Louise Vee

Northern teacher and recently mother to a beautiful miracle baby that she still worries is a figment of her imagination.

Anastasia Vorobyeva

Anastasia Vorobyeva is a performance artist, playback trainer and social activist for human rights. She is the co-founder of VOZDUKH Project of Physical Playback Theatre and is a certified Playback Theatre trainer. And a Vice President of International Playback Theatre Network. Anastasia has created multiple social theatre projects in contemporary and playback theatre around the world including the US, Bangladesh, Nigeria, Lebanon, Asia and throughout Europe as well as projects addressing trauma and social dimension through theatre and art therapy. Anastasia is doing peace building work by writing and teaching long-term projects working with refugees & marginalised communities.

Steven Waling

Steven Waling's latest collection, Disparate Measures 1: Spuds In History, was recently published by Some Roast Poets. He lives in South Manchester. He is published all over the place, and has performed everywhere from Fallowfield to Johannesburg.

Carson Wolfe

Carson explains their inspiration: 'My creative practice seeks to disrupt the page by inviting the unseen to play. I believe that representation is crucial to self-actualisation and I want to carve space for the power of visibility in my work. Therefore, I orbit marginalised narratives like the moon, and always advocate for the gender menaces of the world. I recently graduated with a distinction in English, Writing and Media and was awarded Student of the Year at The Manchester College. I am currently studying Creative Writing at Manchester Metropolitan University, where I am refining my skills as a novelist and poet.'

Mantz Yorke

Mantz lives in Manchester, England. His poems have appeared in print magazines, anthologies and e-magazines in the UK, Ireland, The Netherlands, Israel, Canada, the US, Australia and Hong Kong. His collection 'Voyager' is published by Dempsey & Windle.

www.hiddenvoicepublishing.co.uk

MORE TO COME

STILL WE RISE